P9-CMQ-379

A Children's Museum Activity Book

BUBBLES

A Children's Museum Activity Book

BUBBLES

by Bernie Zubrowski

Illustrated by Joan Drescher

Little, Brown and Company
Boston   Toronto   London

Children's Museum Activity Books in This Series

BUBBLES
BALL-POINT PENS
MILK CARTON BLOCKS

COPYRIGHT © 1979 BY THE CHILDREN'S MUSEUM

ALL RIGHTS RESERVED. NO PART OF THIS BOOK MAY BE REPRODUCED IN ANY
FORM OR BY ANY ELECTRONIC OR MECHANICAL MEANS INCLUDING INFORMATION
STORAGE AND RETRIEVAL SYSTEMS WITHOUT PERMISSION IN WRITING FROM THE
PUBLISHER, EXCEPT BY A REVIEWER WHO MAY QUOTE BRIEF PASSAGES IN A REVIEW.

Library of Congress Cataloging in Publication Data

Zubrowski, Bernie.

   A Children's Museum activity book: Bubbles.
   Bibliography:
   SUMMARY: A guide to having fun with soap bubbles
which includes techniques for blowing and how to make
gigantic bubbles, bubble sculptures, and unusually-shaped
bubbles.
   1. Soap-bubbles—Juvenile literature. [1. Bubbles]
I. Drescher, Joan E. II. Title. III. Series: Boston.
Children's Museum. A Children's Museum activity book.
QC183.Z78   541'.3453   78-27497

ISBN 0-316-98881-2 pbk.

10 9 8 7 6
Published simultaneously in Canada
by Little, Brown & Company (Canada) Limited

PRINTED IN THE UNITED STATES OF AMERICA

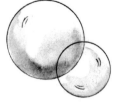

A Children's Museum Activity Book

BUBBLES

INTRODUCTION

People usually blow bubbles in the air using bubble pipes or plastic wands purchased from a store. That isn't the only way to make bubbles. There are many things around your house that can be used to launch bubbles. But bubbles don't have to float in the air; they can also be made in containers on table tops, or on top of all sorts of surfaces. All you need to have fun with bubbles is some dishwashing soap, lots of empty containers, and, perhaps most important, a sense of play.

People often say that play may be fun but it is a waste of time. They forget that Jacques Cousteau

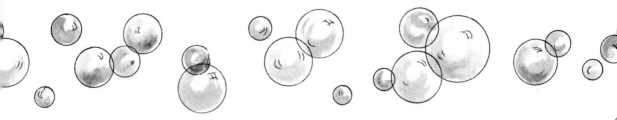

invented the aqualung while playing, and Hero was relaxing when he discovered the principle of the steam engine.

Bubble blowing is great play with the same kind of potential for discovery. Outdoors or indoors, on different surfaces, in different containers or floating free, bubbles display beautiful colors and shapes. But upon closer examination, they also demonstrate some of the shaping forces of nature which scientists have studied for ages.

So while blowing bubbles can be fun, it can also be hard, stimulating work. Making bubble designs on flat surfaces may be a bit difficult at first, but if you practice, you'll soon get the hang of it. Soon you'll be able to play around with this book just the way you do with bubbles. Dip in here and there; find things out; take off on flights of fancy, but most of all, have a good time.

Jar

tray

measuring
spoons

measuring
cup

AJAX
Detergent

STARTING OUT

Because this kind of playing can get quite messy, first you should cover the floor and the table with newspaper or sheets of plastic, or do it in a place you don't mind getting wet.

In a jar, mix a small quantity of dishwashing soap in warm water. Generally, about eight tablespoons of soap to a quart of water is a good solution. The dishwashing soaps which have been found to work the best tend to be the higher priced ones, such as Joy and Ajax. As you gain experience with blowing bubbles, you can experiment with different kinds and amounts of soap, to see which works best for you. Many people think that it is necessary to add glycerine to the solution. This isn't so. Glycerine does help to make strong bubbles, but very big bubbles and long-lasting ones can be made without glycerine if certain procedures are followed.

Using a drinking straw in a shallow tray of soapy water you can produce a great variety of sizes of bubbles. They range from the chains of small bubbles, which you can get simply by blowing through the straw as you move it across the surface of the solution, to large hemispheres that could cover the entire surface of a tray.

Here is one way of making a hemisphere with a drinking straw. Wet with the soap solution the surface you are going to blow the bubble on. Dip one end of the straw into the solution. Hold the straw slightly above the surface and blow gently. You will probably have to try several times before you get the hang of it.

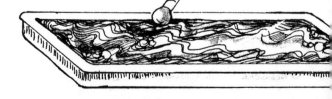

After you've blown a good-sized bubble, maybe the size of half a tennis ball, you can withdraw the straw gently, leaving the bubble behind, or you can try blowing other bubbles inside it.

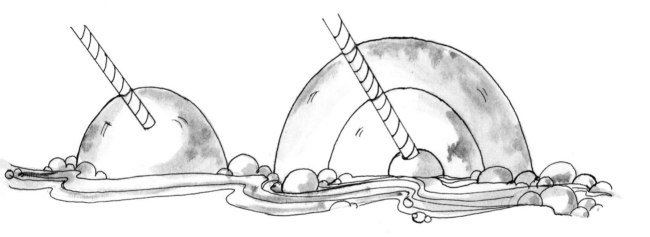

When you have a bubble, touch it with a wet finger, then with a dry one. What happens when you use the dry finger?

You will soon discover that dry places on hands or

other objects that touch your bubbles will make them break. This is because soap films are very thin. When a dry object touches a bubble, the soap film will tend to stick to that object, putting a strain on the surface of the bubble, and the bubble will burst. Remember to keep everything wet; even the sides of the drinking straw.

With practice you will be able to make large bubbles on the table. At first, they might be three or four inches high. What is the largest hemisphere you can make?

BUBBLE TECHNIQUES AND TOOLS

There are all sorts of devices for making bubbles that float in the air. You have probably seen several kinds being sold in stores, such as simple plastic loops. Rather than buying anything, see how inventive you can be in finding interesting launchers. You can use various things from around the kitchen. All an object needs to become a bubble-blowing tool is an opening where a soap film can form. Use tin cans, plastic containers, coat hangers, or pumps (a basting bulb is a simple pump); see how many different ways you can discover for making bubbles. On the following pages are ideas to start with; try them, and see if you can improve on them.

A tube is a basic tool for blowing bubbles. A drinking straw is one kind of tube. A rolled-up piece of paper is another kind. A tin can open at both ends is a very

useful blowing tube. Dip this tube into the soap solution so that you get a soap "window" across one end when you pull it out. Blow gently, but hard enough so that a bubble forms at the end of the can. A twist of the can closes off the bubble and frees it to float in the air.

Since one can works well, why not try making longer tubes? Open both ends of two, or three, or four tin cans and tape them together with masking tape. The end of a longer tube will be farther from your mouth, and the flow of air through it will be smoother. Bubbles blown from longer tubes will be less likely to break. Wider tubes, such as coffee cans, might give bigger bubbles.

VERY BIG BUBBLES

It's exciting to make very large bubbles. Everyone has ideas about what works best for making big bubbles. Generally speaking, when you move devices with large soap-film windows through the air, they will yield big bubbles. Compare a big tube, like one made from two or three tin cans, to a small tube, like a drinking straw. On the end of the straw you get a very small film. Dipping the tin-can tube in soapy water gives you a much bigger film. Using this larger tube, you can make domes on a table top many times bigger than the ones you can make with a drinking straw.

With a tin-can tube you can also produce large free-floating bubbles. First dip one end of the tube into the soapy water and pull it out so that a soap-film window is formed. Blow gently through the tube to make the soap film stretch out. When you have a round or

sausage-shaped bubble, twist the tube to close the bubble off and release it into the air. This twist has to be done in a certain way, so keep practicing until you get it right. You can eventually make floating bubbles as large as a volleyball!

There's another simple device for launching gigantic bubbles that you don't have to blow into at all. To make it you will need two drinking straws and about three feet of light string. Thread the string through both straws and tie the two ends together. Hold one straw in each hand and pull them gently apart to form a frame in the shape of a rectangle. Place this frame in a tray of soapy water, then lift it carefully out so that you have a soap-film window stretched across the rectangle. Be sure that your hands are thoroughly soapy.

Now, holding the frame at arm's length just below your waist, carefully, and at a moderate speed, pull

the frame upward. As you move the frame, a bubble will form. To close it off and make it float, gently bring the two straws together as you swing the frame up. It will take some practice, so keep trying. With this straw-and-string technique, the size of the bubble is limited only by the size of the room and the skill you can develop in moving the frame at the right speed.

BUBBLE SCULPTURE

Here is your chance to be an artist. With the devices and materials already mentioned, try your hand at making sculptures using bubbles. Blow bubbles on top of things, between them, and inside them to see what shapes you can make.

To make a chain of bubbles like the one in the photograph, blow a bubble on the unopened end of a tin can and turn it over, so that the bubble is hanging down. Dip a straw in the solution. Place the tip of the straw in the very bottom of the bubble. Blow very gently. How many bubbles can you add using this technique? What happens to the shape of the chain when you attach the bottom of it to a wet tray?

SOAP-FILM CURVES

If you twist a sheet of soap film in different ways, you can get a variety of interesting curves. The straw-and-string device, which you have used for launching big bubbles (see page 18), makes a good, flexible tool for this activity.

Place the frame in a tray of soap solution. Pull the frame out carefully so that a soap-film window is formed. Twist the two straws in various ways, and see what interesting shapes you can create. Tie the straw-and-string frames in unusual patterns like those below.

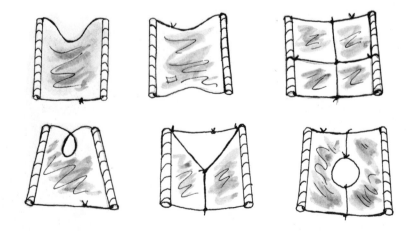

Have a friend make a second straw-and-string frame. What shapes can you make with two frames? Touch the two soap films to each other and then move them slowly apart. Pass one frame through the other.

You can even make a giant straw-and-string frame, six, eight, or ten feet long. Get a friend to take the other end of it. It takes a lot of teamwork, but with care you can make soap films that stretch across an entire room. Watch the film sway as you and your friend move the frame and twist the ends of it. Does the film break all at once, or does the break begin in the middle and travel toward the ends?

SHAPES THAT
MOVE AND CHANGE

There is one more device you can make, which is both an observation chamber and a moving sculpture. You will need a clear plastic cylinder about five inches wide. (This can be made from a piece of flexible plastic wrapped into a tube.) Trim the larger end of a plastic funnel so that it fits snugly into the plastic tube. Place this assembly in a bucket of soapy water so that the neck of the funnel is immersed. Attach one end of a length of standard aquarium tubing to an aquarium pump, or to a balloon which is attached to a plastic ball-point-pen casing. The balloon can be blown up through the pen. Insert the other end of the tubing into the neck of the funnel so that the tubing rests right at the surface of the soap solution, as shown.

As the pump or the balloon feeds air through the tubing, you will see bubbles form inside the funnel

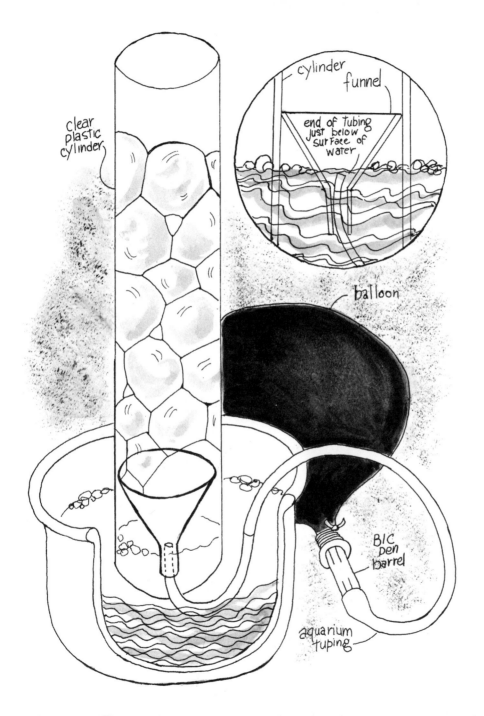

clear
plastic
cylinder

cylinder

funnel

end of tubing
just below
surface of
water

balloon

BIC
pen
barrel

aquarium
tubing

and climb the sides of the plastic tube. If the end of the tubing is below the soapy water, you will get lots of small bubbles; if it is just at the surface, you will get larger bubbles, but fewer of them. Experiment with the tubing by moving it, relative to the surface of the water. Try adding soap to the solution, or adding water to make the solution weaker. Try adding ingredients from the chapter, "Long-Lasting Bubbles," or any other additives you may have discovered.

GEOMETRIC SHAPES

With drinking straws and paper clips, you can make frameworks for soap bubble cubes, pyramids, and other structures. Insert a paper clip into the end of a straw, and slip another paper clip through the first. Place the second paper clip into another straw as shown. Add on more clips and straws to create the shapes you want. It takes six straws to make a pyramid, twelve to make a cube. For most simple geometric shapes, you will not need more than two clips in either end of any one straw.

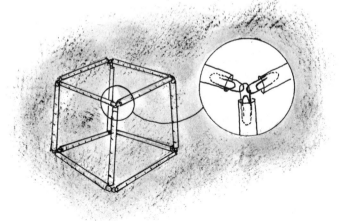

Dip the frames completely into soapy water and pull them out carefully. Touch different sections of the soap film with a dry object. As one section breaks, watch the other films shift and change.

Get some electrical wire, or any other wire that bends easily. Bend the wire into different shapes, such as spirals, knots, and curves. As you dip the shapes into the soap solution, try to imagine what the soap film on each shape will look like before you pull it out.

DOMES AND
OTHER BUBBLE HOUSES

Have you ever seen a building held up by air? It is like a giant balloon cut in half. The walls are made of a strong cloth similar to canvas. The entire skin is supported by air pumped into it. Not many of these structures have ever been used for homes. Most are used as auditoriums or gymnasiums. Someday, though, houses supported by air may become more common.

One person in particular has spent a great deal of time making and studying air-supported structures. His name is Frei Otto. Like most architects, he makes small models of a building before putting up the real one. For models of his dome buildings, he often uses soap bubbles.

The patterns you have already made with soapy water and a drinking straw on a wet surface could be models for dome-shaped structures. You could design your future house using bubbles as your model. With bubbles you can study the ways that walls intersect, the most natural relationships between large bubble rooms and small ones, and the ways that they join

together. You can invent all kinds of special arrangements (for example, a dome inside a dome inside a dome). It's not hard to make a model of one if you remember to keep your straw wet and start each new dome exactly in the middle of the previous one. Another variation is to make a group of domes, like those shown, and add "rooms" next to each other.

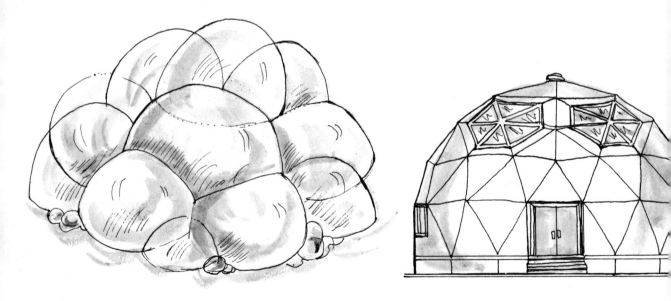

Suppose you wanted to build a house which had curved walls but a flat roof. Bubbles can be used as models for these also, but you will need some extra equipment. You will need a tray, a piece of plastic or glass, and four corks, spools, or other objects which are all the same height and can act as pillars. These pillars will hold the glass or plastic above the soapy water in the tray. (If you are using glass, tape the edges so that you won't cut your fingers.) Fill the tray with liquid about one-third of the way up the corks or spools. Remembering that soap film likes wet surfaces, keep the underside of the glass or plastic and the supports wet. Then, using a long straw or a piece of tubing, blow a bubble between the glass and the surface of the soap solution. The form you will get is a cylinder. Blow one or two more bubbles next to this one and watch them join. What "room" arrangements do you get with two, three, or five bubbles?

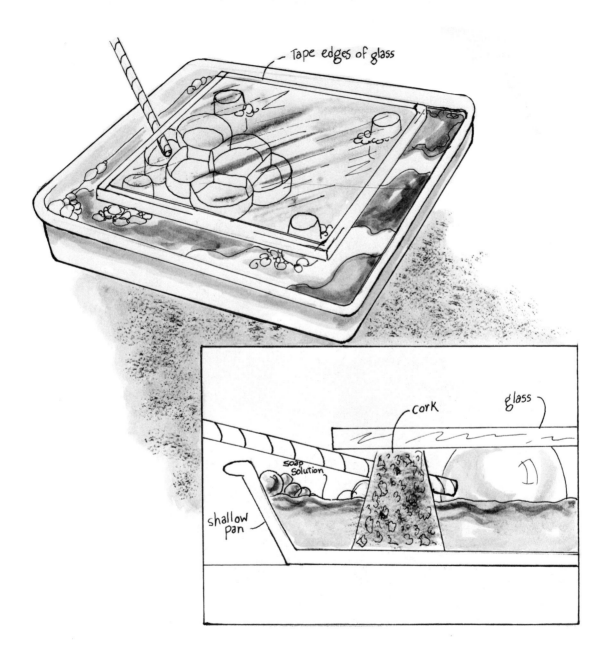

Tape edges of glass

cork

glass

soap solution

shallow pan

BUBBLE BUILDING BLOCKS

Another way to experiment with bubbles as structural units is to create many same-sized bubbles which clump together to form "building blocks." Trying to blow many bubbles all the same size can be difficult, but there are ways of doing it. This section and the next will tell you about devices that make it easier to make uniform bubbles. The following directions show how to construct a machine for making a lot of small bubbles, all the same size.

YOU WILL NEED:

    a large balloon

    a string, about a two-foot length

    standard-size aquarium tubing

    mini-tubing (smaller diameter aquarium tubing,
        available in most aquarium-supply stores)

    adapter (comes in the package of mini-tubing)

Tie the balloon onto the larger tubing. Blow up the balloon through the tubing. Quickly stick the adapter into the larger tubing and insert the small end of the adapter into the mini-tubing. Now the air should be leaking slowly from the end of the mini-tubing. Use a shallow tray filled with soap solution to a depth of about one centimeter. Place the end of the tubing just beneath the surface of the water and move it around. Can you make a straight line of bubbles on the tray?

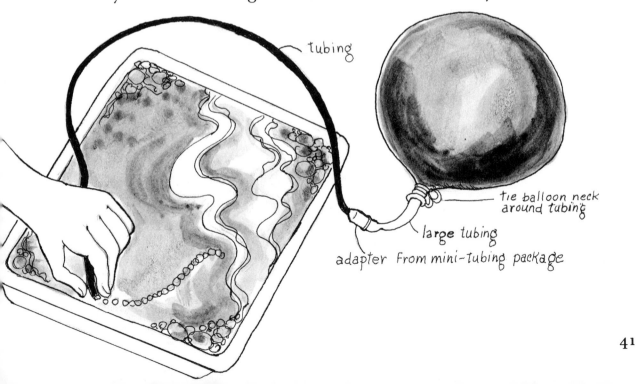

tubing

tie balloon neck around tubing

large tubing

adapter from mini-tubing package

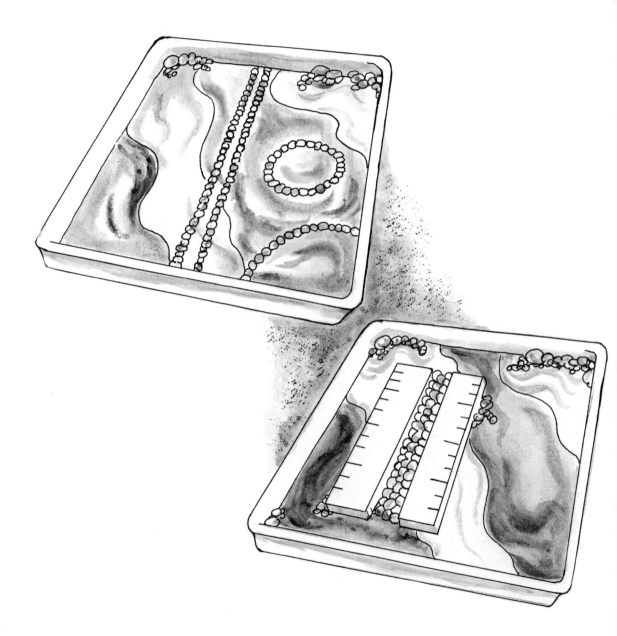

What happens when you make two straight lines of bubbles very close to each other? What happens when you make a circle or curve with bubbles?

Place two wooden rulers or pieces of wood close together in the tray. Fill the space between them with small bubbles. What happens when the two pieces of wood are pulled slowly apart? What other designs can you make? Go back to other parts of this book and see which of the previous activities can be done using the balloon machine.

With two pieces of glass, you can make a glass sandwich filled with bubble building blocks. Separate the two pieces of glass with two strips of wood. Clamp this assembly together using four C-clamps. It is best to place the clamps over the strips of wood, and to place strips of cardboard between the clamps and the glass. The gap between the two pieces of glass should be about a centimeter.

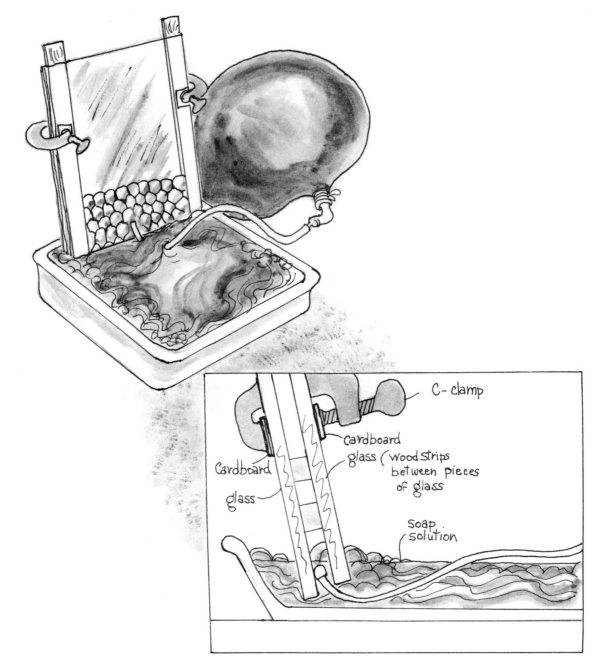

C-clamp

cardboard
glass (wood strips
between pieces
of glass

Cardboard
glass

soap
solution

Rest this glass sandwich so that an open end is in the soap solution. Insert the tubing from the balloon between the pieces of glass just at the surface of the bubble solution. Let the bubbles grow slowly and climb between the glass panes.

The type of "wall" that results may look familiar to you. It is very similar to a honeycomb. You will notice that most of the bubbles in it are six-sided, just as the wax chambers in a beehive have six sides.

Look closely at the sides of all these bubbles, and watch how they intersect. At each meeting point three sides converge. While the bubble walls are forming, you might see four come together briefly, but only very briefly. Four walls meeting at one point is a very unstable situation: one wall is certain to slip away.

BIGGER BUILDING BLOCKS

Six-sided figures, called hexagons, occur where little bubbles all the same size are bunched together. Is this true of larger bubbles as well? Will the same patterns and arrangements develop among big bubbles as among little ones? You can make a device from a funnel and several feet of plastic tubing which will help you to investigate this problem.

Slip one end of the tubing over the end of the funnel. Partially fill a large container (a bucket or dishpan, for instance) with water. Place the free end of the tubing into a tray of soapy water with one hand as you slowly push the funnel to the bottom of the bucket with the other hand. The water which enters the funnel pushes the same volume of air out the other end of the tube each time you plunge the funnel to the bottom of the pail. This means that each separate bubble you form

this way will be exactly the same size as every other one. This also means that any bubble made by plunging the funnel twice into the pail will contain exactly twice as much air as one made from one plunge. Three plunges will make a bubble containing three times as much air as one plunge.

After you have practiced this technique, try making some bubbles in a straight line. Does this arrangement look similar to a line of very small bubbles?

Try making a group of seven bubbles. Do you get a six-sided figure in the middle of the group? Are its sides equal in length?

Using the glass-and-corks platform from page 39, make some large bubbles under the glass. What patterns do you get? If there are no leaks in the connections and no blockage in the tubing, your funnel-and-tubing device should be making bubbles which are all the same size. How can you be sure of this?

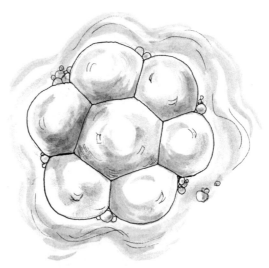

GETTING THE MEASURE OF A BUBBLE

At first, measuring bubbles may seem very difficult, if not impossible. If you keep in mind, however, that soap film can stand being touched, gently, with other wet, soapy objects, then measuring bubbles becomes much easier.

Suppose you want to measure the height of a bubble dome that you have just made. Wet a ruler with soapy water, and carefully lower it into the center of the dome. If you want to measure the width of the dome, slide the wet ruler through the bottom of the dome.

You might want to see if there are relationships between different parts of a bubble. For instance, if the width of the bubble changes a certain amount, does the height change proportionally?

SHRINKING BUBBLES

Soap films have an interesting property that you may have already noticed. When placed in certain kinds of containers or frames, they tend to contract. Because of this tendency, soap films and bubbles take on special shapes and configurations.

There are a number of devices you can use to investigate this phenomenon. For instance, dip a funnel into soapy water, getting it all wet and making a soap film form over the large end. When the neck of the funnel is cleared of all suds and film, what happens to the soap film on the large opening?

Next, form a soap film on a straw-and-string frame. Hold on to one straw as you let the other one hang. What happens?

Now, tie another string across the frame with a loop in the middle of it as in the drawing below.

Dip the frame in soapy water and form a soap window across all three sections of it. What happens to the loop when you break the film inside it while leaving the rest intact?

Finally, take a plastic lid from a coffee can. Poke a hole in the middle of it with a nail. Blow bubble domes of different sizes on the two sides of the lid.

Using a wet, soapy straw, carefully blow away any liquid or film from the hole between the bubbles so that they are connected. What happens to the bubbles? What happens when the two bubbles start off being the same size?

In each of the examples above, the soap film is always trying to pull itself together. Even when the film is flat this will happen. The soap film on the end of a funnel moves to the neck to get to the smallest possible area. This pull is equal in all directions. You saw that when you broke the film inside the string loop. A circle formed each time. Also, the smaller the area, the tighter the film pulled. That is why the small bubble made the big one get larger.

LONG-LASTING BUBBLES

Making bubbles last longer than a few seconds has always been a challenge. Bubble makers have found that by adding certain ingredients to the soap solution and by being very careful, they can make bubbles and soap films that last as long as a few hours. Can you use your experience to select additives and make devices for blowing bubbles which help make longer-lasting bubbles?

First try adding different ingredients to the soap solution to see which ones produce more enduring bubbles. The liquid additive used most often by experienced bubble blowers is glycerine. Divide a soap solution into several containers of the same size. Add a different amount of glycerine to each container, and time a bubble from each solution. Does a larger amount of glycerine give a longer-lasting bubble?

Other ingredients you might want to experiment with are Karo syrup, Jell-O powder, and Certo.

Once you have found a good combination of soap solution and some other substance, try blowing large bubbles and soap films inside a large jar. Remember to wet every part of the inside of the jar with the solution first. Blow bubbles with a long, wet straw to

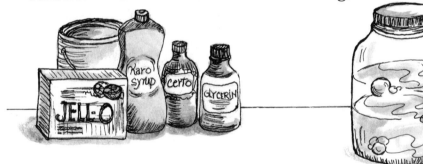

make parallel layers. Each layer will push the one above it farther up in the jar. Put the jar in a place where it will not be disturbed by heat or vibrations.

How long does each layer last? Which layer will break first? Will they last longer on a warm or a cold day?

Here is a review of things to keep in mind when trying for record-breaking bubble longevity:

- When dry surfaces or objects touch a soap film, it breaks immediately. Therefore, before you do anything else, wet the entire surface of the container with which you are working.
- Make sure no dry objects are too near your bubbles. A slight breeze could push the bubble into one, breaking it.
- Very quick bursts of air sometimes stretch a soap film too quickly, causing it to break. A good steady stream of air is best. Wind from a window or from people moving nearby can cause similar problems. Any distortion of a bubble will tend to break it.

58

A CLOSE LOOK
AT BUBBLES

One of the most pleasing aspects of bubble blowing is the range of beautiful colors that appear on soap films and on bubble surfaces. Interesting changes of patterns and textures occur continually on the film of a single bubble or in a group of several as one breaks or another breaks into the group. Bubbles also have interesting reflective properties. Here are some things to look for up close.

- How many different colors can you see in the soap film?
- Do the colors form layers or are they in swirls?
- How do the colors move and change?
- Where have you seen similar kinds of colors in other liquids or mixtures?
- Do the patterns seem to change as you look

at them from different angles, or as the light changes?

Try adding food color to a soap solution.
- Will blue food color give you a blue bubble?
- Does food color alter the colors on the surface of a bubble?

If you have some colored cellophane or plastic, look at a bubble through it.
- Do the colors in the bubble look different from before?

Try looking at bubbles through a pair of polarized sunglasses.
- Do the bubbles change as you turn the glasses in front of your eyes?

While blowing bubbles, you have probably noticed that you can see your face on the soap film.

- How does this reflection compare to one in an ordinary mirror?
- As you move your face close to a bubble, how does the size of the reflected image of your face compare to the reflection of the rest of your body?
- Does the image of your hand change as you move it closer to and farther from the soap film?
- Look at your hand and your face close to a flat soap film such as one that fills a straw-and-string frame. How do they look?

CONCLUSION

Whether you have gone through this book from cover to cover or dipped in here and there, you have found that there is a lot you can do with bubbles. This book is in fact about the game of bubbles. The equipment you have used is limited: soapy water, a straw, and a few containers. The rules of the bubble game are to see how many different shapes or new observations you can make with bubbles using only these limited materials. This book has suggested many ways for you to play the game. Each time you make a group of bubbles you have the chance to add to your knowledge of them. Sometimes you really score when you discover a whole new way of making bubbles or find that watching bubbles has helped you to understand something totally different from bubbles.

There are many discoveries you can still make in the bubble game. One involves discovering the mathematical relationships that come about as you measure bubbles in different arrangements. The manner in which a soap film breaks up light rays is another area of possible investigation. These discoveries are important, but if there is a profit to this book, it lies in making bubbles for the joy of making them, and for their beautiful colors and shapes.

FURTHER READING

For further exploration with soap film:
Boys, Charles Vernon. *Soap Bubbles*. New York: Dover, 1959.

For exploration of some of the mathematical relationships in bubble construction:
Otto, Frei. *Tensile Structures*. Cambridge, Mass.: M.I.T. Press, 1972.
Stevens, Peter S. *Patterns in Nature*. Boston: Little, Brown, 1974.

The books by Frei Otto and Peter Stevens are adult books. The text in each is very complicated. Both books have very fine drawings and photos, however, and a great deal can be learned just by looking at these. Frei Otto's book is especially interesting, showing many kinds of tents and inflatable structures.